Jussa 2 Chics Cooking Healthier in the Kitchen

Copyright © 2019

All right reserved.

No parts of this publication may be reproduced, published in any form, or by any means without the prior permission of the authors.

jussa2chics@gmail.com

Dedication

This book is dedicated to our husbands, Cortez L. Williams, Sr. and James E. Davis, Sr.. You two are a blessing and the funding for our trips. And to our families, this book is the beginning of our health legacy to you.

Special Thanks

A special thanks to our Pastor, Dr. RJ McCowan, for teaching us about a culture of health, Min. Kilzma McCowan Brown for her contribution to our book, and Sonya Sims for facilitating and photographing our first project.

This book will take you on a personal journey of love, laughter and adventure. Lisa and Anna have a very unique approach to presenting new food choices to the African American culture. Their budding friendship has bloomed into something special. These two wonderful ladies met in their local church and realized that they had so much in common. One of the most obvious, was that they both wanted to make lifestyle changes concerning their health. Lisa and Anna began working out together and losing an enormous amount of weight. During the process, Anna experienced some issues with her foot and Lisa would continue to walk in her honor. Their favorite quote was, "My miles are your miles." A true sisterhood was birthed. Anna became a constant prayer partner and support when Lisa started experiencing some health challenges. The two never allowed anything to stop their progress. Their level of perseverance is one to be mirrored. I was so surprised when they announced their "No meat pact". My response was "No meat?" It has been nothing but a blessing to see them reach their goals and maintain such a friendship. I've been inspired along with many others, to make my health a priority and try new foods. This book is sure to make you live, love, and laugh while enjoying a new way of thinking.

Min. Kilzma McCowan Brown

FRAN
/fran/

Noun:

An incredible person that is kind and caring. One who listens and is there in time of need and will be there for you.

Synonyms:

Best Friend, Close Friend, Confidante, Comrade, Companion

Genesis 1:29

And God said, Behold, I have given you every herb bearing seed, which is upon the face of all the earth, and every tree, in the which is the fruit of a tree yielding seed; to you it shall be for meat.

Psalms 103:5

Who satisfieth thy mouth with good things; so that thy youth is renewed like the eagle's.

Proverbs 15:17

Better is a dinner of herbs where love is, than a stalled ox and hatred therewith.

Isaiah 1:19

If ye be willing and obedient, ye shall eat the good of the land:

3 John 1:2

Beloved, I pray that you may prosper in all things and be in health, just as your soul prospers

Abbreviations

GF - Gluten Free

DF - Dairy Free

VEG - Vegetarian

V - Vegan

NON-GMO – Non-genetically modified.

Jussa - Just a

These Recipes Come From Our Heart

Our recipes that we are sharing with you are recipes that we make from our hearts. These recipes are made with love.

We know you will enjoy making these recipes as much as we do.

We have provided you with a variety of vegetarian to vegan recipes which can be changed to fit your taste.

How Jussa 2 was birthed

True story....

Two chics walk into Herban Fix and were amazed at the beautiful and upscale atmosphere of this vegan eatery.

These chics followed the well dressed hostess to a table and sat down with their menus in hand.

Undecided on what to order, they decided to order a lil of EVERYTHING!

The waitress, taken aback by this large order, asked "Are more people coming?"

The two chics giggled and answered *"No. Jussa2."*

Words From Jussa2

Our recipes have the measurements we used but, as far as the yield and preparation time, we really can't say. That part is up to you. Lol.

We could say a dish serves 4 but, we don't know how hungry you are or who in the house has not ate. That 4 servings could easily be 1 and a half.

And, preparation time varies from house to house. You can start and stop to watch your favorite show, get on a phone call, fall asleep, etc.

All we know is that when you're done, your taste buds will be happy.

INDEX

Juices and Smoothie..10-15

Nutty Oats Bowl...19

Spinach and Grits...21

Sweet Potato Wrap..25

Wonton Wrappers..27

Thai Veggie Stir-Fry..29

2 Frans Chili...31

Crockpot Kale Greens..35

Vegan Bibimbap.. 37

Creamy Chickpea and Mushroom Pasta............. 39

Vitamin C Kicker (a juicer is needed for these recipes)

4 Carrots

1/2 Lemon

2 Granny Smith apples

1 Thumb of ginger

4 Stalks of celery

1 teaspoon of tumeric powder

Watermelon Cooler

2-3 cups of Watermelon juice

1/2 lime

1 sprig of mint

Jussa Green Juice

Handful of Spinach and Arugula

Or the greens of your choice
(Use what greens you like)

1 lime

5 stalks of celery

2 Granny Smith Apples

Blueberry Heaven

(Blender/nutri bullet needed for this recipe)

2 cups of frozen wild (organic) blueberries

1 1/2 cups of almond milk

1 banana

1 scoop of protein powder of your

choice 1 tablespoon of flax or chia seeds
(for your omega 3s)

Blend and enjoy!

Blueberries are rich in Antioxidants, fiber, vitamins C, K, and Manganese

P.S. - They are the star of this smoothie.

Just Beet It (a juicer is needed for these recipes)

3 Beets

2 Apples

1 knuckle of ginger

2 Cups of Spinach

Romaine Calm

1 head of Romaine lettuce

2 Apples

4 Orange and yellow mini sweet peppers

1 Jalapeno (seeded)

Storytime.......

Yes, Mama.

We had just left a Mocs football game and was in the mood for some Indian food. We went to a local Indian restaurant and started perusing the menu. Y'all know how some restaurants bring out free bread and butter or chips and salsa before your meal? Well at this restaurant, they bring out chutney and dipping sauce with chips. Lisa and I were tearing it up. Ya' hear me? Tearing it up! We get about halfway through and I ask for some more. The waitress says to me "Eat what is on your plate first." I respond "Yes, mama." Lisa and the waitress burst out laughing. She goes on to tell us how to mix the chutneys and sauces to have a new dining experience. Then a man, whom I assume to be the owner, delivers our food and tells us ANOTHER way to mix the chutney to have a new experience. We didn't want a new experience. We just wanted more chutney. Anyway, our food comes out and we go in on some very tasty Indian food. Everything tasted great but.........we never did get more chutney.

Jussa Juice

A juicer is an investment.

Invest in one.

Your health will thank you.

Nutty Oats Bowl

1 cup of oats of your choice

1 handful of strawberries

1 small handful of walnuts

1 tbsp of chia seeds

1 tbsp of any nut butter of your choice

1 handful of blueberries

Cook oats as directed on packaging.
(Steel cut oats are recommended. Other oats can be used to your taste.)

Place cooked oatmeal in bowl.

Place your fruit in one area on top of the oatmeal.

Place a line of nuts and chia seeds next to fruit.

Add nut butter

You can use whatever fruits, nuts and/or nut butters you like.

Enjoy!

Spinach and Grits

2 cups Old Fashioned grits

Jussa bag of spinach

1 tbsp minced garlic

2 tsp Garlic powder

8 whole garlic cloves

Sriracha sauce

Salt to taste

Boil garlic till soft.

Cook grits to your desired thickness over medium heat. (*Add garlic powder and salt*)

Reduce to a simmer.

Heat your skillet or wok. Add spinach and minced garlic. Saute till desired texture.

Add grits to bowl and top with spinach and garlic cloves. Drizzle with sriracha sauce.

Enjoy!

Storytime.......

Y'ALL AIN'T GOT NO ICE WATER?!!!!!

Early on in out quest to become healthier we would give different vegan/vegetarian restaurants a try. Anna had went to Atlanta visiting her father. While she was there, she found a vegan restaurant that did soul food. She sent me pics of her food (that's what we do) and told me we would visit the original restaurant the next time we're in Atlanta. She hyped it up so much, I couldn't wait to go. Anticipation built as the day came. On our way there we planned on what we were going to order. As we arrived, me being Petty Patty said, "Ummm, this looks a little povertish." Anna says, "Chic, the food is good. Come on!" So, we walked in. Now mind you, Anna had been to their second location so, this was new to both of us. We walk in and FELT the first red flag. It was HOT in there! WE cannot be hot! I was like "Anna!" She looked at me and said "The food is good, though." I was looking suspect at everything. We made it to the food bar. It was scarce because of the "alleged" lunch rush that came before us. The server looked tired, the cook looked tired, and the cashier looked tired. Trying to save the whole situation, Anna asked the server when would they be filling up the greens again. The server, whose scarf was crooked, looked back at Anna and said, "That's it. There is no more coming out." Anna wouldn't look at me cause she knew I was going to say something crazy. We came there to try the greens! We started looking at the few desserts they had, but they weren't all that appealing. All of a sudden a lady walked up to the server looking hot and said. "Can I get some ice water?" The server said, "We ain't got no ice." The older lady put her hands on her hips, bent forward, and said with frustration. "You mean to tell me Y'ALL AIN'T GOT NO ICE WATER?!" The server said "No!" with an attitude. Anna looked at me, I looked at her, and we both walked out of said restaurant. Needless to say, we ended up at Mary Mac Tea Room with 4 sides and 2 meats.

Sweet Potato Wrap

GF Sweet potato wrap

1 Cup of Organic kale *(spinach if desired)*

2-3 Sweet potatoes cut into wedges

1 can of organic black beans *(canned)*

Saute onions and garlic till translucent. Add spinach.

Saute until spinach is tender.

Don't overcook or you will have Jussa teaspoon of spinach!!!

Warm beans as directed.

Roast sweet potatoes in oven till desired softness.

Lay out wrap.

Put desired amount of sweet potatoes in middle of wrap, align desired amount of beans, then spinach. Roll.

Garnish with guacamole or favorite condiment.

Enjoy!

Baked Wontons

1 pack of wonton wrappers

1 head of Napa cabbage *(shredded)*

Jussa bag of bean sprouts

1 cup of carrots *(shredded)*

1/2 lb green beans *(chopped into bite sized pieces)*

4 Green onions *(chopped fine)*

2 tbsp garlic powder and ginger powder

Tamari soy sauce(*to taste*)

Saute veggies together. Add garlic powder and soy sauce.

Let cool.

Preheat oven to 350°

Add mixture on a wonton wrapper. Top with another wonton wrapper. Press edges to seal.

Melt butter.

Brush wontons with butter and bake until the edges are brown and wonton is baked through.

Dipping sauce

Mix 17 oz of Mirin, 15 oz of Tamari sauce, 3 Granny Smith Apples *(sliced)*, ground ginger, garlic powder in a pan over medium heat. Bring to a boil. Lower heat and simmer 2 hrs. Blend in blender for 10 seconds. Yum!

Thai Veggie Stir-Fry

3 squash *(diced)*

3 zucchini *(diced)*

1/2 cup of shredded carrots

3 small red and orange peppers *(sliced)*

1 bag of bean sprouts

3 green onions *(chopped)*

Thai basil leaves (*Add to your taste*)
I love Thai basil so, I added about 12 leaves

2 cups of Jasmine rice

1 cup of sweet soy sauce

Jussa tsp cayenne pepper

Cook Rice *(set aside)*

Heat skillet/wok

Add all veggies and cook until desired doneness

Add sweet soy sauce and cayenne pepper

Mix vegetables

Serve immediately over rice

Enjoy!

2 Frans Chili

3 cups pinto beans
(dried packaged or organic canned)

64 oz organic vegetable broth

2 onions *(diced)*

2 tbsp minced garlic

1 tbsp cumin

1 - 28 oz can diced tomatoes

1 - 15 oz can seasoned tomato sauce
(chili seasoned)

2 – 8 oz pks of Ancient Harvest Organic Quinoa

2 - 1.25 oz pks of Brooks Chili Seasoning (GF)

Cook 3 cups of dried pinto beans per package directions OR 3 cups of organic cooked pinto beans canned.

Add all ingredients together and stir with beans of your choice

Cook for 45 minutes over low heat

Enjoy!

Storytime.......

THE LIL' GREEN HIDE AWAY

We were in Nashville looking for a good vegan restaurant. After a not so good experience, we now looked for the number of stars and good reviews before we picked one. We thought we had found one. It was new and the reviews were good. We were starving so, we went on over. First of all, we passed by it, it was so small. When we found it, Anna looked at me. Parking was in the back and so was the outdoor seating. It was a lil cool outside so I said, "It's too cold to sit outside." We sat in the car debating on whether to stay or go. Anna, who is always willing to give a place a shot, made an executive decision to stay. My granddaughter and her headed in while I parked. As I get out of the car, I notice two men arguing. One was a delivery driver, the other was the cook of the restaurant. I said to myself "Oh, no. This is not good."

I pass the two men arguing, walk up to the door, open it, and there sits Anna and my granddaughter in a tight and cramped little room. It's lime green with 1 small table and 2 chairs. Anna saw the look on my face. She looked at Zaccheah and said "Let's go."

We got in the car and laughed all the way to P.F. Changs.

Oh, yeah!!!

How to reach Jussa2

Find us on FB: Jussa 2

Subscribe to us on YouTube: Jussa 2 Chics

Email: jussa2chics@gmail.com

And, yes. We respond back.

Now back to the recipes......

Crockpot Kale Greens

1 bag of kale Greens *(12 oz)*

1 1/2 red peppers

1/2 green pepper

1 large onion

1 tomato

2 - 32 oz boxes organic vegetable broth

3 tsp of minced garlic

2 tbsp liquid smoke

1 tbsp smoked paprika

2 tbsp apple cider vinegar

Pink Himalayan *(salt to taste)*

2 tbsp Amino Bragg's liquid Amino

2 tbsp Hot sauce *(optional)*

Rinse greens thoroughly if desired

Saute peppers, onions, and tomatoes together

Add remaining ingredients and stir

Place in crockpot

Cook on low heat for 6 hours.

Enjoy!

FRANS VEGAN BIBIMBAP!!!

Simple... Quick... VERY TASTY...

2 cups – Rice *(be adventurous and use a flavored rice like jasmine)*

1 - 13.7 oz pk Gardein Beefless Ground *(seasoned and heated with smoked paprika, ground cayenne, and garlic powder)*

1 large Onion –Dice onion and saute with minced garlic

Portabella mushrooms - Saute with minced garlic and a pinch of seasoning salt

1 - 14 oz jar spicy or regular Kimchi

1 cup - Raw Greenleaf lettuce

1/2 cup of cilantro

Arrange it separately on top of rice. Mix all ingredients together

After mixing, top with your favorite sauce *(Tamari or low sodium soy sauce, sweet thai chili sauce, sriracha sauce or of your choosing)*

Note:
Using your favorite seasoning to saute the vegetables is the key to flavoring this dish.

Yum Yum!

Creamy Chickpea and Mushroom Pasta

2 cans - Garbanzo beans drained *(save liquid of 1 can)*

1 - 16 oz pkg of spaghetti noodles

2 cups – Heavy whipping cream

1 cup - Vegetable broth

1 pkg - Portabella mushrooms *(fresh)*

1 - Yellow onion

1 can - Diced tomatoes *(your favorite flavor)*

1 pkg - Field Roast Sausage *(Italian)*

1 tsp - Cumin

1 tbsp - Coriander

1 tbsp - Smoked Paprika

1 tsp - Lemon Pepper

1/2 tsp - Cayenne pepper

Salt to taste

Season the saved garbanzo bean liquid with the cumin, coriander, and lemon pepper. Place the garbanzo beans in the liquid, stir and let them marinate for 30 minutes.

Cook sausage per package instructions

Cook spaghetti and drain

Saute onions and mushrooms over medium heat in cayenne pepper, salt, and smoked paprika until tender

Add garbanzo beans with seasoned liquid

Heat to a boil

Add vegetable broth and heavy whipping cream. Bring to a second boil

Add tomatoes, spaghetti, and field roast sausage

Add noodles and mix thoroughly

Lower heat and top with parsley

Enjoy!

Lisa Davis True Story…

"WHOA!!! Mrs. Davis, your blood pressure is 230/101!!!! Your blood pressure is at stroke level!" The nurse said as she looked at me with concern. I was on a hospital bed in the emergency room. All I could think about was my husband, kids, and my grandbabies....MY GRANDBABIES!!!! THEY ALL NEED ME AND I NEED TO BE NEEDED!!!!!! I was fighting tears and fears. I texted one of the head Ministers/Sister Friend at my church for her agreement that I'm healed and this blood pressure go down right now in Jesus name!!! She responded immediately and set her faith in agreement with mine. After several hours, the doctors (yes with an s more than one) got it down to 176/90 but, they were looking concerned when I left. They told me to follow up with my primary care physician. After several months of this happening, I went through doctor after and blood pressure med after blood pressure med. The doctors did the best they knew to do. One doctor told me, "I've done all I know to do. I'm going to refer you to another doctor." I asked God to give me wisdom about my body. After all, He created it! I finally realized at the end of the day, I had to take some responsibility about my own health. The meds they put me on lowered my blood pressure but, I could not handle the side effects. Seeing what the meds do to some of your organs over time was not good either. After seeing Forks over Knives, Super Juice Me, Eating You Alive, and other documentaries, I started doing research on health and nutrition. I learned a lot of my health issues (i.e. heart palpitations, stomach problems, I had my gallbladder removed, but if I knew then what I knew now, I wouldn't have had it removed) could be controlled, if not eliminated, by what I ate. Through elimination of some foods, continuing to walk and hitting the gym when I had time, I started my journey to a healthier lifestyle. I eat A LOT of fruits and veggies (Organic as much as possible). I juice and do green smoothies as well. I eat very little meat (fish if any). I'm really aiming for a meat free diet. I have lost 90 lbs by eating this way. When I started, I was on three blood pressure meds. Now, I'm down to a low dose of 1 every other day. GLORY BE TO GOD!!! I confess healing scriptures over me every morning and I started taking supplements as well. B12, D3, and probiotics.

My results are not typical.

TAKE YOUR MEDS until you are released by a professional doctor. Everyone's body is different. Good doctors can and have saved many lives!!!! I encourage you to do your own research about your condition. Find you a doctor who is willing to work with you in nutrition as well as medicine.

Integrative medicine, naturopathic, and holistic are a good place to start. Even with that, do your research for a good one. Prevention is far better than trying to find a cure any day. Remember at the end of the day YOU are responsible for your health and the maintenance of it!!!

God Bless

Lisa

Jussa Few Words From Anna

Yesterday doesn't matter. Today is the day that matters. Start from where you are. Starting today, make a effort to eat better. You may have fell off the wagon but, that's okay. We've all been there. But, guess what? Jump back on and keep it moving. I'm living it right now and I will continue to live it.

Jussa2 Rule #3

If you find a healthy dish you love, it's okay to eat it over and over and over until your palette wants something different. Cause let me tell you, those green beans from P.F. Changs and avocados kept me happy for a while.

When we decided to do this cookbook we immediately knew it would be more than just recipes. We wanted to show you our franship and some of our adventures. More importantly, we had people who were starting their healthy eating journey in mind. Hence, these great recipes. Jussa2 is about living life, having fun, and enjoying great eats that are good for us and to us.

God Bless
Anna

MEDICAL DISCLAIMER

We are not a health care practitioners. ALL information you read in this book is purely for informational and educational purposes. Information is not intended to treat, cure, or prevent any disease. Statements within this site have not been approved by the FDA, meaning information and statements regarding health claims in this book have not been evaluated by the Food and Drug Administration. These stories and testimonies are solely our personal experiences and opinions and should not be interpreted as an attempt to offer a medical opinion. The writer{s} or publisher{s} of this site are not responsible for any adverse reactions, effects, or consequences resulting from the use of any recipes or suggestions herein or procedures undertaken hereafter. If you have questions about food, diet, nutrition, natural remedies or holistic health, please do your own research and consult with your health care practitioner. If you are pregnant, nursing, have a medical condition or are taking any medications, please consult your health care practitioner before making any changes to your diet or supplement regimen.

Made in the USA
Columbia, SC
08 February 2020